Hair!

Written by Erin Howard
Illustrated by Alessandra Micheletti

raintree
a Capstone company — publishers for children

Jill is going to town on the bus. She meets Annika and Annika's dad at the bus stop.

"My mum has cut my hair for me until now. But not today," Jill tells them. "Today, I am going to the shop for a haircut." They sit on the top deck of the bus so they can see the shops as they go by. Then Annika's dad sees the stop they need.

"We all have to get off here," he says, pressing the button.

"Oh, 'Hair Here'. That says it all!" says Jill.

"I will come with you, Jill," Annika says. "Dad is going to the pet groomers on the corner to pick our dog up."
"I wish I had a dog," sighs Jill.
"I will be with you soon," the hairdresser, Stella, tells Jill.
"Let's look at this book," Annika says to Jill. "It is on hair, from far back till now."

Annika points at a picture. "Look at that old coin," she says. "Her hair has short curls and a net. She must have been important to be put on a coin!"

"That dog has short curls, too," Jill says.

"Yes, she has had a good trim at the groomers," says Annika.

Annika looks at the next picture. "She must have been important, too. She has braids and silver chains in her hair."
"I bet she had a maid to do her hair," Jill says. "She must have been rich."
"The silver chains will have cost a lot, as well," Annika says.

"That's a cool dog. The groomers cut his coat short," Jill adds.

"I can tell you like short hair. But look here. Rich men had long curls in 1700," says Annika. "I think they must have worn wigs."

"Yes, it says they were 'powdered wigs'. Powder stopped them smelling," Jill says. "Oh dear, this one had rags twisted in her hair to get it to curl," Annika tells Jill. "She had to have them in all night long!"

"That must have hurt. I bet she was cross in the morning!" says Jill. "Oh, do you see that labrador? His short fur looks smart. No curls for him."

Then Jill says, "Look at this picture. They are from Japan. They look smart, too."
"It took all morning to do that sort of hair," says Annika.
"I bet that dog's haircut took all morning, too," says Jill. "Its fur gets long and thick. It is too hot for it in the summer unless it is trimmed."

Jill is still waiting for her turn in the hairdresser's chair. She sees a boxer dog jog by with a man. The man has short brown hair and the dog has short brown fur.

"They are a good pair," thinks Jill.

Now it is Jill's turn for a haircut. She hops up into the chair. Stella puts a cloth on her.

"This will stop your neck and back getting wet. Now, how much shall I cut off?" she says, pulling out a curl.

Jill says, "Well, it is long and thick, and will be too hot in summer!" She thinks for a bit. "Can you cut this much off?" Stella nods, wets her hair, then snips and cuts. Soon there is a lot of cut hair to sweep up.

Jill points, "I like the zigzag in that man's hair."

"Yes," says Stella, "and he will be back next week to have it trimmed, and the next, and the next!"

They hear the clippers go buzz, buzz.

Jill sighs. She feels a bit sad. What will her mum think when she sees her hair? "It is so hard to tell that my hair has been cut," she tells Stella. "It will be 'Jill, was it good in town? It is chicken for dinner.' And that will be that!"
"You are right," says Stella. "You cannot tell I have cut your hair as it curls up. But I have a plan!"

Stella puts wax in Jill's hair. Now it is smoother.

Then, starting near the top, she puts it in a thick braid and slots a silver band on.

"What do you think?" says Stella.
"This braid is a bit like the one in the book we looked at!" says Jill.
"It will be cool in the summer like that," says Annika.
"Yes, there was no need for me to have it cut too short today!" says Jill.

They all go back on the bus.
Jill's mum frowns. "Is Jill with you, Annika?"
"Yes, this is me!" says Jill.
"So it is!" says Mum. "Your hair looks so good!"
Jill grins. "Thanks. And when I go next, I might have it a bit shorter!"